Time to
Move
South
for
Winter

For Dad. Love you to the moon and back (three times!) – C.H.W.
For my fellow bird enthusiasts Emma Levey and Emma Lockley! – J.L.

First published 2021 by Nosy Crow Ltd
The Crow's Nest, 14 Baden Place
Crosby Row, London SE1 1YW
www.nosycrow.com

ISBN 978 1 78800 813 6

Nosy Crow and associated logos are trademarks
and/or registered trademarks of Nosy Crow Ltd

Text © Clare Helen Welsh 2021
Illustrations © Jenny Løvlie 2021

The rights of Clare Helen Welsh to be identified as the author and Jenny Løvlie
to be identified as the illustrator of this work have been asserted.

A CIP catalogue record for this book is available from the British Library.

Printed in China
Papers used by Nosy Crow are made from wood grown in sustainable forests.

1 3 5 7 9 8 6 4 2

Time to Move South for Winter

Clare Helen Welsh   Jenny Løvlie

nosy crow

On the cold, glassy waters of the Arctic,
the sun seemed a little less bright.
The sky seemed a little less blue.
A touch of frost settled along the rocky, sandy shore.

A tiny black-capped tern opened her wings.

Up . . .

up . . .

up she flew . . .

in search of summer in the sky.

It was time to move
south for winter.

The little tern spotted whales below,
rising like islands in the ice-filled sea.

She dipped down to watch them breaking through
the rolling waves and blowing spray up into the misty air.
A cold winter wind began to howl.

The giants dived a little deeper
beneath the surface.

Down, down, down the whales swam,
in search of summer in the waves.

It was time to move south for winter.

The tiny tern spied caribou, snaking like ants over
the hills, between the valleys and through rivers.
She flew down towards them, following their tracks
over the wintering ground.

On, on, on the caribou climbed,
in search of summer in the hills.

It was time to move south for winter.

A flock of geese flew past, soaring like planes on the wild winter wind. The tiny tern tried her best to keep up. But their giant wings glided effortlessly on the thrill of the storm.

Over, over, over the geese soared,
in search of summer on the lake.

It was time to move south for winter.

Off the coast, the tern spotted a turtle,
its front flippers powering across the open sea.
But no sooner had she seen it, than the soft-topped,
tear-drop turtle disappeared deep into the ocean,
looking for jellyfish in the warm water currents.

Down, down, down the turtle dived,
in search of summer in the ocean.

It was time to move south for winter.

Suddenly, the tiny tern found herself caught in a kaleidoscope
of colour and wings. A canvas of black and orange, black and orange.
Beating in their millions, butterflies sailed the cool winter breeze,
on the promise of shelter in the tall fir trees.

Round, round, round the butterflies fluttered,
in search of summer in the trees.

It was time to move south for winter.

The tiny tern stopped to rest her weary head.
She ruffled her grey and white feathers and
stretched her little legs . . .

but she knew she couldn't stay.
The tiny tern opened her wings.

Up . . .

up . . .

up she swooped . . .

Further, further, further still . . .

until . . .

. . . she saw a colony of little black caps, just like her.

The Arctic terns were nesting
in nooks and snoozing in crannies.

They had all moved south for winter.

The tiny black-capped tern folded her wings.
Finally, it was time to rest in her rocky, sunny
home on the Antarctic shore.

But when long, sunny days . . .

make way for cold,
dark nights . . .

then it will be time
for the not-so-tiny tern . . .

to head back to the brighter
northern skies . . .

and have a tiny
tern of her own.

Time to move north for summer.

Migration is when an animal moves from one place to another in search of a new home to live in for part of the year. Animals migrate for many different reasons, such as to find food and have babies, but all the creatures in this book leave a cold place for a warmer one.

Arctic terns make the longest migration of any animal in the world. During the Arctic summer they live in the north, but each year as winter draws near, they fly south for the long, warmer days of the Antarctic summer. The journey south can take up to three months. When they return to the north, the terns have chicks. Young Arctic terns have dark bills (beaks) and reddish-black legs, but as they get older, their legs and bills turn bright red. In their lifetime, a single tern flies the equivalent distance of three trips to the Moon and back.

Humpback whales migrate to tropical seas to have their babies when the water in the Arctic and Antarctic begins to freeze. In summer, they travel back to the cold water of the North and South Poles to feed on plankton, krill and fish. Until then, they get energy from fat stores known as blubber.

Caribou live on the North American coast but when the first snow falls, they migrate south inland, where it is warmer. The herds feed on lichen, which is a plant that grows on rocks. When summer arrives, the caribou return to the north, travelling up to 950 kilometres – that's almost the length of Great Britain. Caribou make the longest migration of any land animal.

Canada geese fly south for winter to the warmer parts of America and Mexico, when their North American homes freeze and there isn't enough food. They glide in a skein, which is a V-shape that allows them to travel further and for longer without getting as tired.

Leatherback turtles are the largest of all turtles. They migrate over 6,000 kilometres between the cooler Canadian waters, where they feed on jellyfish, and warmer nesting grounds in South America and the Caribbean. They live alone, but in the summer all the female turtles come ashore to lay eggs. The tiny baby turtles hatch on the beaches and begin their lives in the ocean.

Monarch butterflies travel 4,500 kilometres every autumn from North America down to the mountain forests of Mexico. When they arrive, they huddle together on the branches of fir trees. In the spring, they return north again. A monarch butterfly doesn't live as long as some other animals, so each butterfly only ever makes one part of this journey.